Watch it Grow

A Bee's Life

Nancy Dickmann

Raintree

www.raintreepublishers.co.uk

Visit our website to find out
more information about
Raintree books.

To order:

☎ Phone 0845 6044371

▤ Fax +44 (0) 1865 312263

▨ Email myorders@raintreepublishers.co.uk

Customers from outside the UK please telephone +44 1865 312262

Raintree is an imprint of Capstone Global Library Limited,
a company incorporated in England and Wales having its
registered office at 7 Pilgrim Street, London, EC4V 6LB
– Registered company number: 6695582

Edited by Nancy Dickmann, Rebecca Rissman, and Catherine Veitch
Designed by Joanna Hinton-Malivoire
Picture research by Mica Brancic
Production by Victoria Fitzgerald
Originated by Capstone Global Library Ltd
Printed and bound in China by South China Printing Company Ltd

ISBN 978 0 431 19536 0
14 13 12 11 10
10 9 8 7 6 5 4 3 2 1

British Library Cataloguing in Publication Data
Dickmann, Nancy.
Bee. -- (Watch it grow)
571.8'15799-dc22

Acknowledgements
We would would like to thank the following for permission to reproduce
photographs: Shutterstock p. **4** (© Monkey Business Images); © NHPA p. **18**
(Stephen Dalton); iStockphoto pp. **5** (© James Brey), **7** (© stachu343),
8 (© mikerogal), **9** (© Viktor Fischer), **11** (© stachu343), **16** (© Serdar
Yagci), **17** (© Dainis Derics), **19** (Proxyminder), **22 left** (Proxyminder),
22 right (© stachu343), **23 middle bottom** (© Dainis Derics), **23 top**
(© stachu343); Nature Picture Library p. **20** (© Kim Taylor); Photolibrary
pp. **6** (© Oxford Scientific (OSF)), **10** (age fotostock/© Don Johnston),
12 (Juniors Bildarchiv), **13** (Oxford Scientific (OSF)), **14** (Animals Animals/
© Anthony Bannister), **15** (Oxford Scientific (OSF)), **21** (Phototake
Science/© Scott Camazine), **22 top** (© Oxford Scientific (OSF)), **22
bottom** (Animals Animals/© Anthony Bannister), **23 middle top** (Oxford
Scientific (OSF)), **23 bottom** (Phototake Science/© Scott Camazine).

Front cover photograph (main) of bees on a dandelion reproduced with
permission of iStockphoto (proxyminder). Front cover photograph (inset)
of a worker bee taking care of larvae reproduced with permission of
iStockphoto (stachu343). Back cover photograph of a worker bee taking
care of larvae reproduced with permission of iStockphoto (© stachu343).

The publisher would like to thank Nancy Harris for her assistance in the
preparation of this book.

Every effort has been made to contact copyright holders of material
reproduced in this book. Any omissions will be rectified in subsequent
printings if notice is given to the publisher.

Contents

Life cycles

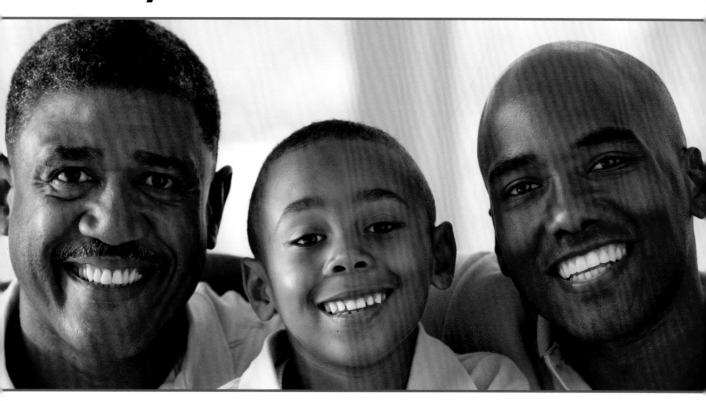

All living things have a life cycle.

Bees have a life cycle.

egg

A bee hatches from an egg.
Then it grows up.

young bee

A bee looks after young bees.
Later it will die.

Eggs and larvae

nest

Bees live in a nest.

cell

Each hole in the nest is called a cell.

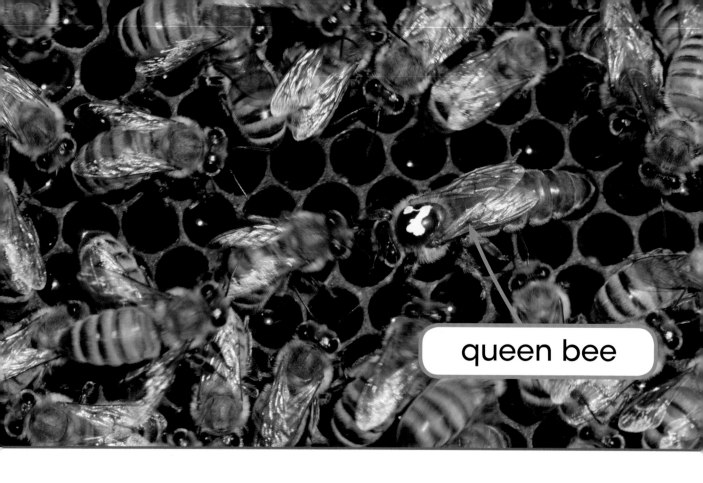

queen bee

A queen bee lays eggs in the cells.

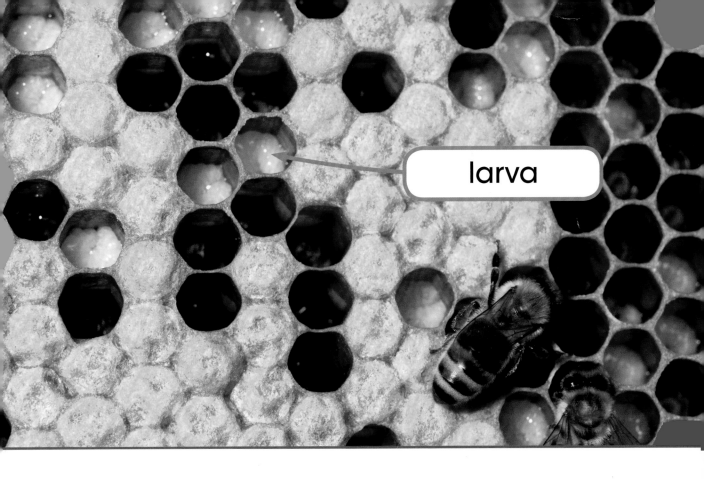

larva

A larva hatches from each egg.

Becoming a bee

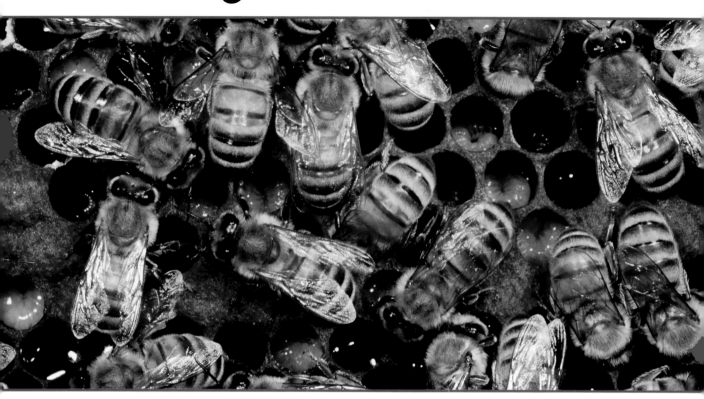

Older bees feed the larva.

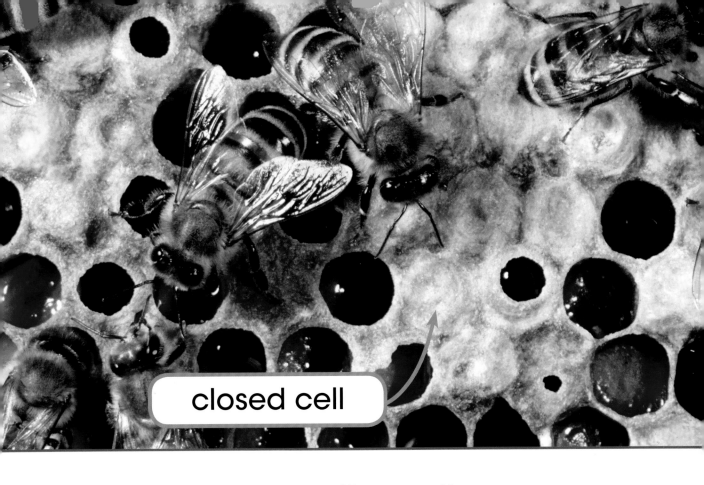

closed cell

The bees close up the cell.

The larva changes into a bee.

The bee then comes out of the cell.

Workers, drones, and queens

Most larvae grow into worker bees.
Worker bees get food.

honey

Worker bees make honey for
the larvae.

worker bee

drone bee

Some larvae grow into drone bees.
Drone bees do not work.

queen bee

Some larvae grow into queen bees.

queen bee

A queen bee lays eggs.

larvae

The life cycle starts again.

Life cycle of a bee

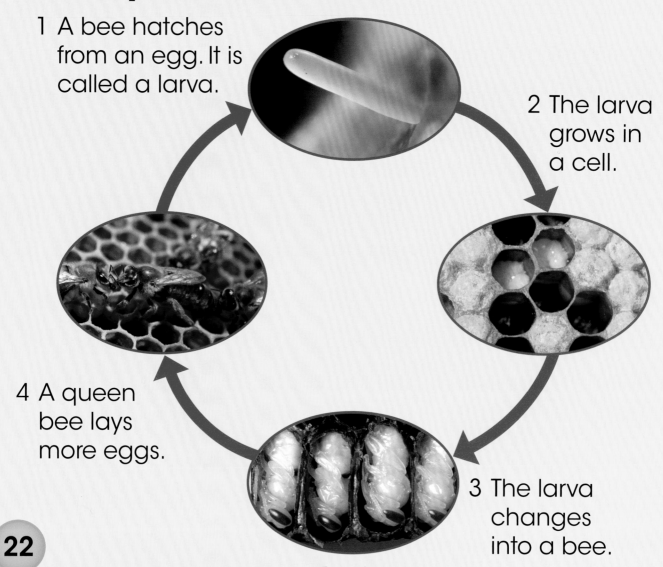

1 A bee hatches from an egg. It is called a larva.

2 The larva grows in a cell.

3 The larva changes into a bee.

4 A queen bee lays more eggs.

Picture glossary

cell small hole in a bee's nest. Larvae live in some cells. Other cells store honey.

hatch be born from an egg

honey sweet liquid that bees make to feed their young

larva (larvae if there is more than one) young form of an insect, such as a bee. Larvae do not look like adults.

Index

Notes to parents and teachers
Before reading
Ask the children if they know what a baby dog is called. Then see if they can name a baby cat, horse, cow, sheep, and pig. Do they know what a bee's baby is called? Do they know what a baby bee looks like? Talk about how some animal babies look like small versions of the adults and some animal babies look very different.

After reading
• Talk to the children about how bees defend themselves. Explain that they only sting if they are bothered – otherwise they leave people alone. Try to make a list of other animals that sting or bite to defend themselves.

• Bring some different types of honey for the children to taste. Discuss how honey tastes different because of the flowers that the bees that made it visited. Let the children do a taste test of each honey to see which they like best and make a tally chart to record the result. You could make honey sandwiches for a healthy snack.